TAP YOUR TRAUMA AWAY:

using EFT to counter the emotional impact of childhood trauma and abuse

by Tanya Lovett, Advanced EFT Practitioner and Matrix Reimprinting Practitioner

FOREWORD
Karl Dawson

EFT Founding Master and Creator of Matrix Reimprinting

I am always excited to hear new accounts of EFT and Matrix. Both have been a huge part of my life and I am grateful for that. I have seen both create remarkable change and healing for so many people and am happy that this book continues to spread the news about the power and capabilities of these techniques.

Tanya has captured the essence of the techniques and shown that they have the capacity to make a difference to issues such as grief, loss, low self esteem and drug addiction as a consequence of sexual abuse. None of these are easy topics to face but EFT and Matrix can handle them with grace and relative ease, reducing the power of their impact and their ability to affect an individual's life well after the initial triggering event.

If you are suffering from the effects of limiting beliefs and decisions you made in childhood or early adulthood or just know life isn't the way you want it to be, I invite you to read these stories and consider whether EFT or Matrix might be techniques that could release you too.

Tanya Lovett

I hope you take hope from this book; even the biggest
of issues need not hold you in their grip any longer,
now you have been introduced to tapping.

I wish you well

Karl

INTRODUCTION

This book contains the EFT stories of four women, a chapter in their lives. It could have been four men but I just happened to work with four women at around the same time. All four experienced loss or trauma in childhood that was still affecting them in adulthood. All four used EFT or tapping to change their adulthood. I have asked them if I can tell their stories in order that others can decide whether they think EFT – or its extension Matrix Reimprinting – might help them live fuller and richer lives.

And just to note, it is only a chapter in their lives. Like all of us, they are still on their lifelong journey so I am not claiming they are fixed, just that they have released something that has helped them move to a better place in which they are more true to themselves and less blocked. And that that release can have a hugely important and positive impact in the present.

So what is EFT?

EFT stands for Emotional Freedom Techniques. It is a means by which a person reduces or eliminates the negative emotional impact of an event. It involves tapping on acupuncture or acupressure points in a sequence whilst focussing on the experience that was traumatic – whether it was a trauma as everyone would see it or just traumatic to that person. The sequence is nearly always the same, the tapping is gentle but you can feel it and brain scans show that this tapping calms activity in the amygdala, the primitive part of the brain which relates to the now well-known fight, flight or freeze response, allowing new perspectives on a a situation following the calm. A phrase, known as the set-up phrase, helps the person tune in to their issue at the beginning of each sequence and then short phrases that keep the person focussed on an aspect of the issue are spoken as each acupoint is tapped, which can change the brain activity in relation to this aspect of the issue. In all these stories the trauma is big; sexual abuse, loss, neglect. But especially if it happens when we are children, the traumas that can affect us may not be noticed by someone else; it may that an unkind word, a taunt, a dismissive gesture could have been experienced as traumatic.

EFT is a gentle process which involves "creeping up on the problem", diffusing emotions as soon as they arise rather than re-traumatising the person. This doesn't mean there aren't tears sometimes but the tapping releases the emotion quickly so the individual is soon able to view the experience calmly and without strong emotion.

EFT was developed by Gary Craig after he learned TFT (Thought Field Therapy) from Roger Callahan and decided it could be simplified. Roger Callahan developed TFT following striking success using acupoint tapping with a woman he had been treating for an extremely severe water phobia for 18 months using his existing therapeutic skills but with only limited effect. The tapping cleared the phobia in a few minutes. (An account of this story can easily be found on the internet - Roger Callahan Origins of TFT)

Gary Craig simplified TFT and created EFT which can be learnt and used by anyone. (Gary has developed EFT further and is now working with a model called The Unseen Therapist, which you may be interested in exploring, but his original manual can be found here.) TFT and EFT have had striking results with many conditions and there is now a large and growing evidence base, including randomised controlled trials (RCTs), which demonstrate tapping techniques are effective at reducing the effects of PTSD, anxiety and depression. But there are also many case examples of it being used for almost anything from physical pain, through addictions to phobias. If you have a condition you can probably find a case example of someone finding success using EFT to combat it. This is not to say that it will work on anything but Gary Craig's thinking was to "try it on anything" as there are no reported side effects and it might just work for you. He wouldn't guarantee success – he would always say, "we don't know if it will work"- but he always recommended trying as often it did work. If you have the money, I would go and see a practitioner and get some deep shifts quickly and with support. If you don't, listen to some of the many online tap along sessions and see if they can make a difference for you. (Here's one of mine.)

So what is Matrix Reimprinting?

Matrix Reimprinting was developed by Karl Dawson who is one of the EFT masters trained by Gary Craig. In Matrix, Karl uses EFT to work with what he calls our ECHOs – stuck or trapped parts of ourselves that have frozen because of a trauma. His thinking is that we all have many ECHOs which we are often unaware of but which affect our functioning in the present. They are usually the root of beliefs or decisions we have made and still live by, such as 'I am unlovable' or 'it's safer to withdraw from others', and using EFT with the ECHO that made this decision or formed the belief and then changing the memory can allow us to live differently, free from that limitation in the present. It's an amazingly powerful technique.

And who am I?

I trained as a mental health nurse and have worked with adolescents with mental health difficulties and in both community and inpatient adult eating disorder services. I still work for the NHS for Hertfordshire Partnership University NHS Foundation Trust but my EFT work is entirely separate from my NHS work and is neither endorsed nor supported by HPFT. I trained as an EFT practitioner in 2010, as an Advanced Practitioner in 2015 and as a Matrix Reimprinting Practitioner in 2017. I work in Hertfordshire,

UK and online specialising in EFT and Matrix work with women in their 30s, 40s and 50s who are still held back by the effects of childhood trauma and abuse.

I invite you to read the stories of these four women and hear how these techniques impacted positively on their lives. I invite you to consider whether you too are impacted by events in your childhood. Or just to look at your life today and if it is not the way you would like it to be, if you are not living in a way that is positive and enlivening both for you and the world around you, then maybe EFT or Matrix could free you to be more fully you, to be happier and healthier and to enrich the world. Some people might feel nervous about the responsibility of enriching the world but please don't worry. If you free yourself from past negatives and live true to your inner wisdom, if you live by the truth that you are unique and therefore can affect the world in a unique way just by being you, you <u>will</u> enhance the world. First you will impact those people around you and then that will have an impact on the people that their lives touch – which can then impact thousands or millions of people that you never actually know! But all you need to do is just be you, the freed, empowered you!

But let's start with you. Could you use EFT or Matrix to free yourself and live a fuller and richer life? Have a read and see what you think.

G LOSSARY or EXPLANATION of TERMS USED

<u>"tapping on" or "tapped on"</u> Tapping with the fingers of one hand on the sequence of acupuncture points whilst focussing on an issue. The issue is what is tapped on eg p.4 "we tapped on her fear"

In order to **<u>"tune in"</u>** to the issue an EFT Practitioner will ask the person to describe any sensation in their body when they think of the event or emotion and describe what it feels or looks like eg p.4 the fear was a "heaviness...in her stomach and chest" and then changes to a "sensation in her throat". Colour and shape can be used to describe the sensation further if it helps the person connect with the issue they want to work on.

<u>Intensity</u> – EFT reduces the experienced strength of an emotion or physical pain. This is often measured using a <u>SUDS scale</u> (Subjective Unit of Distress Scale) which is a measure developed by Joseph Wolfe in 1969. It has been used in cognitive-behavioural treatments for anxiety disorders (e.g. exposure practices and hierarchy) and for research purposes and is used regularly by EFT practitioners. In the SUDS scale 10 is the most intense the experience of the emotion, memory or pain could be, 0 is where there is no emotion or intensity at all. The aim of EFT would be to reduce the intensity to 0 or 1 whenever possible before moving on to another aspect of the experience.
*Reference: Wolpe, Joseph (1969), The Practice of Behavior Therapy, New York: Pergamon Press, **ISBN 0080065635***

<u>"aspects"</u> A great deal of attention is paid in an EFT session to aspects of an event or experience. This may include different feelings, different views of a memory or different elements of a pain. For example, a person may feel anger when first thinking about something but as the anger clears will begin to feel a sadness or loss. EFT would be concerned to deal with the anger as fully as possible before moving on to the sadness so that unacknowledged anger didn't resurface later. Or it might be that a fear of spiders is initially present when the person looks at a picture and the anxiety subsides but an aspect of the fear is the spider moving so tapping would have to be done whilst focussing on the movement of a spider as well as the static picture.

The Movie Technique is a specific EFT technique used to approach an event gently and without diving into strong feelings. The most intense section of an event such as the impact in a car accident or the moment a person was told of a death etc is imagined as a film. The film is given a title and the person is invited to rate the level of intensity of any feeling experienced when thinking just about the title and reducing that intensity before beginning to play the film. Following this and as the film is played in the imagination, it is stopped as soon as an intensity is experienced and that feeling becomes the focus of the tapping. Once all the points of intensity have reduced, the film is replayed to check if there are feelings left. New feelings are ofte experienced once the initial ones are acknowledged and dealt with. The film is worked on until there is no strong emotion experienced whilst replaying it in the imagination.

Monthly group sessions EFT can be done in a group setting. I have run groups monthly which seems a frequency that people are able to commit to, although others will run groups at other intervals. The monthly sessions either focus on a particular topic which everyone brings their own associations to – so we might focus on fears or phobias, money concerns, relationship issues etc - or each individual will bring an issue they want to work on in that session. In a group the focus usually rotates from one person to another and others tap at the same time. Using the principle of Borrowing Benefits, people are able to move forward with their own issues even if the words used aren't personal to them. The effectiveness of EFT seems to come from focussing on an issue, and the words help this happen, but if the person is tuned in to their issue, the words aren't always necessary or the words reflect common experiences so allow people to tune in to different issues at the same time. And sometimes the words designed to focus on someone else's issue can resonate and cause release for the individual who is tapping, is tuned in to what they want to work on but isn't the subject of the tapping round. See EFT Universe's explanation: https://www.eftuniverse.com/borrowing-benefits

<u>A session or a set of EFT sessions:</u> An EFT session with me lasts an hour whether it's online or in person. This seems to be a good amount of time to make a difference but not too long for the client. It can be that people feel quite tired after a session and it's probably best not to have any longer than an hour as a regular session. (A one off session can sometimes last longer if the person wants to clear a lot.)

Typically before a first session the client would complete a questionnaire so that I have an idea of their goals for our work. If not I will ask them what they want from the work at the beginning of the first session following discussion of the disclaimer. The disclaimer is an agreement that the person will not stop any medical treatment without consulting their medical professional and looks at confidentiality and data protection. Some EFT professionals physically tap on their clients but I ask the client to tap on themselves and only tap on them - if I have their consent - if they would prefer or if they are in a process in which it is easier for them to focus on the issue without having to concentrate on the actual tapping. However I generally like the person to tap on themselves because they are then confident to use the techniques between sessions which will speed up and enhance the process.

Following this I typically introduce the person to EFT through focussing on how they are feeling in the moment. This allows the person to experience EFT before exploring a more difficult issue. The next stage is to guide the person to focus on the issue they have come with, tell me about any emotions and physical sensations that arise as they focus, see what their earliest connection with this sensation or emotion is and then rate this sensation or emotion out of 10. We will then begin a round of tapping or move into Matrix, asking the adult self to meet the younger self in the memory in question. Rounds of tapping would continue until that particular sensation or emotion is reduced to 0 or 1 in intensity. Then we would explore another aspect of the memory or move on to another memory. There are different techniques that may be used. With Matrix, after reimprinting we would ask the younger self if there were other connected memories in which the same emotion or sensation was experienced and move to that memory. The process would continue for the duration of the session.

Future sessions would start from where the person is when they arrive and I ask them to focus on where they want to be. Sometimes as well people bring thoughts and connections that have been made between sessions.

It is difficult to say how many sessions a person will need. It will vary. I think it's important to remember that therapy such as CBT or psychodynamic therapy which can address the same kind of issues as EFT, can last for months or even years. EFT is generally a quicker process and people can find resolution in two or three sessions and I recommend that people have at least three sessions, but it for many people it takes longer and often people start with three or six and then choose to continue for longer as they realise what EFT can bring to other areas of their lives.

E FT WITH ANNABEL

It struck me as so cruel when I read her initial form. She had nursed her dying mother and then, without explanation, her mother left all of her belongings to her sister.

Annabel came to me because she had to run a workshop and she was incredibly anxious about it. She was running it in place of her own tutor and she was so conscious that her tutor's were big shoes to fill. Would people be disappointed that it was her taking the course rather than the tutor who had such an enviable reputation? Would they reject her from the start? Would she be able to teach the same way, to communicate as her tutor did? Although she wasn't conscious of it then, a script was playing in her head – that of trying and trying to be as good as her sister but in her mother's eyes, never being so. This was repeating now - she was afraid she just couldn't, that she was incapable of, being good enough.

EFT for Annabel worked first on the immediate situation. She had a workshop to run that weekend and she was petrified. We tapped on* her fear, first of all experienced as a heaviness located in her stomach and chest. With tapping, the intensity went reduced and she was left with a sensation in her throat. I asked her when she remembered first feeling this throat sensation. She remembered a time when she was about 3 and some shelves fell towards her. She was saved by the wall which prevented the shelves actually crushing her, but she cut her leg and was shocked by the noise and near miss. She may also have realised the enormity of the fact that this was a shelf unit full of ornaments that her mother used to clean every day and were clearly hugely important to her. What consequence would come from displacing and probably breaking these treasures? For whatever reason, this little girl didn't receive a soothing hug from her mother but was hit and sent upstairs to her room to nurse her wound and her shock alone. I say, "for whatever reason": EFT can help people move to a place of acceptance or even forgiveness of another. It was not right that Annabel wasn't soothed or comforted but it is likely that the mother, in this case, had received little care herself so she had few resources. In one of the Tapping Solution videos, Nick Ortner has a great metaphor of an energy bank. We might have 1000 pounds or dollars of energy at birth but as 'life happens' and perhaps we are criticised or belittled and are left to cope alone using our own resources, we pay out from that bank of energy. Instead of receiving care and cuddles which would be mean no payment was due or may increase our bank balance, people without care have their energy resources drained. Thinking about painful moments, replaying them in our minds, takes further deposits. If we do not have enough positive energy moments that repay energy back into our account, we go overdrawn or bankrupt. Stress, overwhelm or illness are often the result.

So in Annabel's case, it is possible that her mother had too few deposits and too many withdrawals in her energy bank and therefore did not have the capacity to give to her child. Now it's not a passive process and there will have been times Annabel's mother will have had choices: whether to stay in draining relationships; whether to continue to dwell on childhood sufferings as an adult; whether to see situations like the shelf falling as a personal assault and insult or an accident in which a little girl is hurt. But our capacity to make the better choice can be severely limited by our experiences, particularly our early ones.

The most helpful aspect of this viewpoint when used within EFT is that it's possible to play with options through words which enable the client to stop blaming themselves and to interrupt the assumption that they must have been a bad person for the parent / significant other to reject them in that way. We can also be freed from resentment which always holds people down. So if we were tapping on Annabel's memory we might start with the thoughts: "I'm so angry at mum/mummy" "How dare she hit me and leave me on my own when I was hurt" "I was only three" "I was shocked and she didn't realise" "I was hurt and all she did was scream at me and send me to my room" and even something like, "I hate/hated her so much". The anger may then change to sadness, sadness for that lonely moment and perhaps sadness for the overall lack of closeness with the mother. So then we might refocus the tapping on: "I felt so alone" "I was scared and didn't know how to make myself better" "I needed to be held". And at some time we can bring in the possibilities (and I love the word 'maybe' in EFT as it can gently open a new perspective). "Maybe she didn't know what to do herself" "Maybe she hadn't been parented". But of course this might not be true so you would be likely to follow straight away with: "Of course she knew" "Everyone knows that little children need hugs when they are hurt" "But maybe she wasn't hugged" "Maybe she's doing what was done to her" "Well, she should know better then" "She should know it hurts" "Maybe I wasn't a bad person" "Actually adults get it wrong sometimes" "I didn't know that when I was 3".

Tapping on this memory allowed Annabel to give voice to some of the anger and sadness she had felt in that moment. It also allowed her to reconnect with the resourceful little girl that she was. Instead of wallowing in her feelings, what the three year old had actually done was climb over her baby sister's pram which was in the way of the window and escape to her favourite spot in the garden, playing without her mother knowing she was no longer in her room. When we checked back to the sensation in her throat, there was hardly any of the sensation left, she felt confident to speak, she had given voice to the thoughts that had in effect been trapped inside her and she was in touch with the spirit of the three year old self who wasn't going to let life bring her down but would play regardless.

The first session with Annabel was enough for her to hold the workshop with minimal nerves. It was actually fairly difficult as there were some people expecting Annabel's tutor, but she handled it so well the participants asked for a second day.

In her second session, we looked more deeply at her relationship with her mother as Annabel had experienced recurrent depression and thought the two were probably connected. We began by tuning in to the way she felt when she was depressed. This very quickly brought her to a memory of her mother not speaking to her for a week when she was 8. Her mother would often punish Annabel by being silent, but this was the longest this punishment had lasted.

The experience of a week was too long for the EFT movie technique* so we just homed in on the feelings Annabel had when she remembered that week. We tapped while tuning in to her overwhelm which then became sadness. Finally she felt indignation; it was unfair that her mother treated her like this. Once the intensity reduces it's possible for EFT to lead the person to other memories and Annabel realised then that she was also indignant- and sad- at a memory of when she was 13 and happy and her mother's silence had crushed her. We were able to find this memory easily because it connected emotionally with the first memory and were able to work on that as well. With depression, there are usually a series of memories that need to be dealt with so I didn't expect that we would have relieved the depression in that one session. However with EFT it is usual that dealing with a number of memories means that, after a time, the emotional impact of others just collapses without also having to deal with them directly.

Sometimes experiences in sessions spill out into the intervening period, which is why it is brilliant that EFT is simple enough to be used by the person on their own, when feelings arise. Annabel felt angry after the session and the next day she met up with a friend and found her controlling. Her friend may or may not have been controlling and if she was, may or may not have been any more controlling than normal. What was probably happening was that Annabel was allowing herself to become more aware of the extent to which her childhood was controlled by her mother's moods and judgements and she was therefore, probably temporarily less tolerant of others' behaviour. She had tapped during the week to keep the feelings under control but was quickly back in touch with them when we talked about them in the next session. So we tapped again on her feelings of anger. She realised there was a connection with her last session; she felt judged by this friend, felt that her friend saw her as "not good enough" just like her mother. She experienced a ball of anger at her core, a feeling that soon became linked to the obligation she felt to nurse her mother when she was dying. But as she tapped the ball dissipated; instead she was left with emptiness and sadness.

Anger often covers grief and sadness. Annabel felt sad at the lack of happiness in her childhood, she felt sad at the "not good enough" burden she had carried all her life. Annabel could have resented the angry feeling rising up towards her friend and blamed the tapping and withdrawn. If she had she wouldn't have got in touch with the grief and sadness underneath. In all good therapeutic experiences there is usually a time when negative feelings become clearer to the person and it's only if they stay with the process that the feelings lose their intensity and become a less powerful presence. If they are shied away from and buried again, they will continue to have an unconscious influence, and unhealthy behaviours and patterns will persist. The beauty of EFT is that negative feelings are rarely experienced for long. In Annabel's case, by using EFT the empty sadness soon became a light headedness which she understood to be a good feeling, a freedom in which she no longer had to carry her burden.

We did tap to ground her at the end of the session to ensure the light-headed freedom became embodied as an experience. It only took a couple of tapping rounds for her to experience a sense of excitement and creativity and an openness to being more true to herself, to being Annabel.

Annabel's process of becoming true to herself and free from the burden of her past was, and probably still is, ongoing. She would feel frustrated at knowing what she wanted and sometimes reaching it but then fall back into her old patterns. By the time we're well into adulthood we have experienced much that we understand as reinforcement of early beliefs and fears. EFT, sometimes gradually, sometimes incredibly quickly, can reduce the intensity of those beliefs so our behaviour changes as a consequence. But the number of experiences we have had by adulthood may mean that a bit of persistence is needed to clear enough of the emotional burdens as is necessary. In the next few sessions, the heaviness in Annabel's core returned and as we tapped the sensation moved up into her throat and there was a catch in her voice when she said aloud, "I'm not good enough". This was the beginning of a new voice emerging that was protesting at the old. She was beginning to prefer the freedom and new sense of self to the familiar "not good enough" place in which she held herself back and limited herself. There were more memories that needed working through, some from adulthood when she had had panic attacks because she feared and expected criticism, resulting in overwhelm. She began to realise she might need to be kinder to herself and at one point realised that her mother might have had some good intentions. Her mother was fearful of the world – for whatever reason – and she may possibly have been trying to protect her daughter from a world she saw as frightening. The trouble was – well one trouble was – she did it by giving her daughter the impression that she was 'wrong' and 'at fault' rather than teaching her how to take care of herself and cope with the perceived dangers in the world.

One session illustrated this. Annabel remembered not understanding what the point of school was, what school was for when she first went. It seems that because her parents were themselves frightened of the teachers, they had avoided talking to Annabel about school and preparing her for it. The "world" was so frightening it couldn't even be spoken of. Yet the young Annabel had to go out into it anyway and often felt wrong and odd. The following session we asked the little Annabel, who we had tapped with by imagining her, or by connecting with her in the Matrix, what she wanted to say to her mother. She said, "The world isn't scary but exciting and I want to enjoy what it offers".

In the last session the constant dread in Annabel's stomach had gone. It was still there in relation to specific events but was much closer to a "normal" nervousness that anyone might feel. By the last session – we had had only eight hour-long sessions – Annabel realised that the tiny blocks to confidence and freedom she continued to experience, were actually blocks she was putting there herself, in order that she would have an excuse to fail. Nelson Mandela's inaugural speech written by Marianne Williamson, famously stated that it is not failure but success that people fear. (I have a blog post that quotes this passage) This was true for Annabel. She visualised letting her blocks float away down a river. The open space devoid of blocks felt weird to her at first, but at the end of our course of sessions, she knew she could choose not to put the blocks back in her way, she could choose to strengthen her belief that the world is exciting rather than scary and she could allow herself to enjoy success, success in which she was being true to herself.

This is how Annabel put it:

I came to Tanya initially, because I was concerned about my anxiety around a public speaking event and to see if she could help with my recurring depression. ... After just one session, I left feeling confident and ready for the forthcoming event, which went very well as a result. [Following that I worked] through some of the deep-seated issues associated with my depression. Consequently, I am feeling much lighter and happier. ... my results have been amazing.

E FT WITH CLAIRE

Claire decided to book a six session package as she was ready to change. She was in the middle of a divorce and knew that generally she wasn't being true to herself. In her words, she was ready "to live a fulfilling life and follow my heart/soul mission."

But to do this she needed to face "demons", relics from a troubled childhood that continued to affect and determine her actions as an adult. And there were many events that she had to contend with. An alcoholic and abusive father, a mother who did not stop the abuse, parents who struggled to show affection and give attention, bullying throughout primary and secondary school, a sexual assault by a medical professional when she was 13, the death of her brother by suicide when he was 15 and she was 17 and into adulthood, a bad car accident in her mid-20s, post-natal depression, her husband's affair which resulted in a child and the on and off confusing attentions of a "soul mate" who caused as much pain as joy. With all those events, I was glad to be using EFT which usually works faster than other therapeutic techniques and although there are often tears in sessions, they quickly dissipate and the person doesn't become retraumatised.

As is usual in my EFT work, I asked Claire what was most important to her at present in order to decide where we should start. She decided her first focus was on what she described as pain and love in her heart. She rated this pain as an 8 or 9*. It was a big pain – but connected with big love. This theme recurred throughout our work; a desire to love constantly being knocked back into pain.

The first connection we made to this was a sense of abandonment powerfully felt by Claire as a young girl. She remembered waiting at school in the place they had arranged, to meet the boy she later identified as her soul mate for their first kiss, only for him not to turn up. She experienced excitement about the love developing, followed quickly by a disappointed and embarrassed pain. Often connections are made in EFT sessions, either by asking the person when else they have experienced the feeling being worked on or just by another memory popping up, and we quickly moved to a younger Claire, desperately disappointed by her father who had promised her a holiday with her nan but had never delivered. And the earliest memory in that session was that of her mother's face as she watched Claire being hit by her father but did nothing; the little Claire hoping for love, experiencing abandonment and feeling perhaps the strongest deepest pain of these three memories. Abandonment and a sense that good things never quite come to her repeat through Claire's story, right into the present. For a child, such memories quickly become a belief about not deserving good things, it being difficult to understand that in fact the adults might be getting it wrong. At this point, using EFT was enough to reduce the strength of emotion that Claire felt whilst remembering these events.

I used Matrix Reimprinting as well as EFT with Claire. Using Matrix beginning with the love/pain feeling, Claire got in touch with a memory of a visit to a zoo when she was three. I'm not sure if she knows whether it was an actual memory but through imagining herself stepping into the memory, she looked at her mother and quickly understood that she felt empty of love herself because her own mother had died when she was young. She imagined bringing a host of female ancestors into the memory which resulted in mother being loved and looked after and freed Claire from the responsibility she had felt to fill that emptiness for her mother, even at the age of 3.

Remember Karl Dawson believes that making a difference to the memory means making a difference to the present. The younger self or the memory of the younger self can be released from the stuck situation and it no longer exists as a stuck situation in the present, no longer holding the person back. Once mum was OK, we asked the little Claire what she needed. She said she felt trapped and wanted to get out of the fenced area of the zoo she was in but didn't know how. At that point she knew she wanted her father or her soulmate to help her, but other than holding her hand, they appeared unable to help. So she simply stepped just outside the enclosure herself. We had reached the end of the session so I checked in with Claire. She was ok to leave it there with a new understanding of her mother and connection to and compassion for her younger self.

What can happen between sessions is that buried feelings emerge and further processing of memories can occur. Mid-week Claire had a surge of loneliness and grief but she said it quickly resolved and she felt at peace. At the beginning of the next session, Claire said the three year old her was still just outside the zoo enclosure but was OK there unlike in the last session when she felt uncomfortable and wanted to move away. She seemed to be doing what I have experienced using Matrix Reimprinting, that a very young self in a memory appears to wait for her other memories and experiences to resolve. When they do, the little self understands the future is safe and can move on.

Matrix Reimprinting work really does seem to show that experiences from earlier in our lives get stuck without us realising and the belief or decision that we created at that time directs our life. This zoo memory was connected to Claire's belief that good things never quite happen to her and in particular that she will never be able to rely on anyone else.

A technique in Matrix is to ask the subject of the current memory whether there's anywhere else they think needs attention and the memories are invariably linked in terms of their theme. During this session the young Claire asked the "now-Claire" to go to a memory of her "stealing" money for sweets when she was 6. The little Claire was never given nice things and when she found some money on the way home from school and bought herself sweets, she was so happy. However her mother found out the money wasn't hers and threatened to call the police. How scary for a six year old.

Another memory followed of 2 year old Claire with a new baby brother. She sang and danced when he first came home – indeed she had told everyone in the hospital that she had a new baby brother – but when she was at home, the joy stopped abruptly when her mother found her doing a poo in the corner of the room. The little Claire was told off severely. Talking to the young Claire using Matrix she said she didn't really know how to use the toilet yet and her parents were so preoccupied with her brother, they hadn't attended to her needs. Claire was forming a belief – in her two year old brain – that joy was limited and had boundaries and if she was happy, that happiness would soon end. Similarly a memory the two year old took us to which reinforced this belief was of Claire coming home from school, aged 7, really happy and wanting to tell her mother about her day. For some reason, and the little Claire didn't know if it was an accident or deliberate, within a few moments of entering the house and happily talking about her day, Claire's mother had burnt her with an iron. Her happiness again was abruptly and violently destroyed.

So through our work, Claire's understanding of her childhood story was refined. She gradually realised that it wasn't that good things didn't come to her but that if they came, they had some-times – and at significant times - been abruptly and often pain-fully taken away. This had meant that she had often decided that it was better not to allow herself happiness, or at least be very cautious around it when she began to experience it. In adult life, this had resulted in her driving good experiences away or mis-trusting them. She also began to understand that her experience of happiness being short-lived, was often due to the struggles of others, not because it was in any way inevitable that happiness had to be short-lived for her. This allowed her to let in and appreciate happiness when it appeared and begin to nurture and protect it.

Through our Matrix work we went into all those memories, told the little Claire she was a lovely little girl and her happiness was brilliant and perfect. We brought in loving resources and people to share, appreciate and complete her happiness and support the idea that she could enjoy love. Claire rated her unconditional love of herself higher after this work.

But then she began to test it further. Her "soul mate", the person she had wanted to kiss as a teenager, had been a constant presence in her life but she had never quite allowed herself to trust and enjoy this relationship. But her current marriage had ended – she was going through a divorce because her husband had had an affair that had resulted in a child – so she was free to try again.

Stefan (the soul mate) was in Germany and Claire was in England but they did begin a serious relationship during the time we worked together. There was beauty in this relationship and Claire absorbed and enjoyed the depth of his love, but she often found herself jealous and mistrusting. We had to tap on the overwhelming mixed up feelings as well as visit other memories in which men – and particularly her father – had made promises and let her down. Or where love – or maybe attention which often feels better than nothing – became abusive. Claire was scared to trust and commit herself because she had known abuse through her life, so we worked through her imagination to open new possibilities, in particular the possibility of loving herself and being truly loved by another. EFT involves words which allow the client to focus on the memories and emotions that are troubling, and the tapping on the acupuncture points is understood to calm the brain activity in the amygdala which occurs when an emotional threat is experienced. This process seems to allow many memories to be addressed more quickly than when tapping isn't used.

Abuse from her father was physical and violent but there were other painful memories that involved men or males. The death of her brother was the subject of one session. The worst feeling when Claire focussed on this was the knowledge that she couldn't rescue him. Her current self accompanied her younger self through the memory of travelling to see her brother "at peace" – she knew he had been tormented – just after she had been told of his death. Claire's younger self felt safer as we travelled through the memory, because she knew she was not alone and Claire began to realise she was holding a feeling of guilt, the guilt at not rescuing her brother, which linked with a sense of guilt for having done a poo after her brother's birth and guilt at "stealing" sweets. On this occasion Claire's mother was a resource. She came into the earliest memory and talked to the 2 year old Claire, explaining that she loved her but that her baby brother would need more of her parents' time for a while. Through tapping whilst focussing on all these memories and the emotions Claire felt whilst remembering (which in effect are the emotions that were still having an impact on her life), Claire eventually realised the guilt wasn't hers and she was allowed to let it go. She decided to give it to some angels, having packaged it up. It did take her a while to let it go because the little her didn't think she deserved love and a knot of fear in her stomach was identified as being a fear of who she would be without the guilt. But with tapping, the knot loosened, she was able to let go of the guilt package and she felt calmer.

Forgiveness came into the sessions too. Forgiveness is often difficult. We blame ourselves at some level for much of what happens in our lives. We continue to punish ourselves years after the event. Or we stay angry at others when they have treated us badly; the anger might be reasonable but holding on to the emotion only serves to cause further damage to ourselves. We are often unaware of whether the other person remembers the incident or feels the guilt , and we are _never_ able to control what they feel and whether they are in fact still suffering. Forgiveness only came at the end of our work and before that stage, Claire shifted her thinking and beliefs.

In another session we had been able to change the memory of the abuse from the medical professional, a hospital professional – Claire wasn't sure what his role was – by empowering Claire to say no. It didn't happen straight away; she first pictured herself questioning him as to why he wanted her to perform the action that resulted in abuse but still did what he asked. She then accepted help from her adult self who came into the memory and helped her younger self report the man. He was arrested and handcuffed and in the new image she was supported by her ancestors. Eventually she decided to go and talk to the man by herself, let him know that he had taken away part of her childhood and tell him how angry and disgusted she was at his actions. At the point she had talked to him and returned to the waiting room, she really began to feel a pure love that she was able to take into her heart and into her body. In a previous session we had worked on filling the hole he had left in her childhood with pure love but she was only able to feel truly congruent with this once she had given him back responsibility for the experience. To explain a bit further, I had previously asked Claire how she felt once we had worked on this memory; she said she felt he had left a deep hole inside her. I then asked her what she wanted to feel and she said she wanted to feel love there instead. So we tapped whist saying "Even though I feel this deep hole inside me when I remember this experience, I choose to fill it with love". At the point we first did this Claire could accept this experience of love to some extent but it was only when she had envisioned giving him responsibility for the event and stopped thinking she must be in some way to blame that she was able to experience a strong acceptance of that sense of love. Claire still didn't feel drawn to look at forgiveness in this memory but she did let her younger and therefore her current self know that she could now choose her own beliefs about men and sex that weren't determined by her past and by others actions and beliefs.

In the final session Claire said her relationship with her soulmate was "amazing". It wasn't perfect but deep and real. As she had wanted, she was able to love despite the myriad events of her life. She said she had let go of the anger she had felt about her past. Forgiveness sometimes can just be realising it's possible and good to let go of anger. And Claire said she now looked at her past with love and healing. She could feel compassion for the bullies at school, understanding that whilst their actions were not right, they came from a place of pain and damage that needed love and healing too. At times during our sessions she had felt safe and this sense of safety and peace had allowed her to send happiness and healing to her childhood house, which was never really a happy place, and to others. Claire finished her sessions when she knew it was time to leave the country, join her soulmate and take a job that involved her being true to herself. It was not that there was nothing left from her past to heal but she felt whole and strong enough to trust where she should go next, to a place of greater peace and fulfilment. Her journey continues but she has let go of much that limited her sense of what was possible for her in her life. As she continues to grow, she is doing so with a deeper self love and trust in making good judgements about the love she can receive from others.

EFT WITH CATHERINE

Catherine told me that she had had a happy childhood until the age of 7. Then a devastating event occurred. That and its consequences changed her whole future, her sense of safety and security in life and her ability to feel safe within herself. At this age Catherine's mother had her first grand mal epileptic seizure when Catherine's dad was out and she was at home with her mother and younger sisters. Catherine was terrified. She thought her mum was dying and some of our later work was focussed on the fear she had felt when seeing her mother's contorted face that continued to affect the focus of her energy well into her adult life. Catherine told her sisters to stay in the house and ran shoeless in the thunder and lightning outside, bringing back a neighbour who was a doctor. Catherine's father later praised her for her actions but what she "knew" was that she had simply fled, unable to bear the scene. This disconnect with Dad was never spoken about but at that moment Catherine formed the belief that she was a fraud, not a hero as she was portrayed. She did run to a neighbour but she said she was running away, not to get help; she did find a doctor but she said she had just knocked on doors indiscriminately and it was luck that the neighbour she found was a doctor; and she did come back with the neighbour – despite her fear – but she didn't think that was at all noteworthy. She also formed a belief that she was a coward, a coward who couldn't face the frightening scene.

After that Catherine's mother had epileptic fits every six months or less but Catherine and her sisters lived in fear of them. From that time Catherine was afraid to be alone with the person she most loved and needed. Her world had turned upside down. And when Catherine's mother died when she was 14 – she was found to be suffering with a brain tumour – she felt desperately alone, lost and different, a feeling that stayed with her into adulthood.

Catherine's mother's death impacted both her experience of school and her ability to learn. She felt different – other children had mothers – and she felt a deep sense of loneliness resulting in a struggle to understand what she was being taught. In adulthood she was diagnosed with dyslexia but whether her struggle with learning would have developed whatever her childhood experience or whether it was a result of the trauma, fear, aloneness and deep loss which gave her little capacity and energy to focus on school work from an early stage of her formal education, she will never know. The dyslexia diagnosis, when it came at the age of 45, was a relief as it made sense of her struggles at school. Her disappointment when her neat workbooks became messy and half finished had an explanation. But it also confirmed to her that she thought differently from others, and didn't take away her pain and a sense that she was stupid, when others - and this was in adulthood - laughed at her inability to do things.

Our work began with Catherine's memory of finding her mother, being terrified and fleeing. She judged herself harshly for her actions and her fear of this memory was 6 on the SUDS scale*. We tapped on* accepting herself, which is part of the EFT protocol anyway and then used Matrix Reimprinting to bring her grandparents into the memory so that they could take charge and look after both Catherine's mother and the children. In this memory Catherine ended up on the swing in the garden feeling (more) secure. However she was still worried.

We (rechecked) the memory and Catherine's young self brought us to the recent past. Catherine could see she had good friends, a brilliant fiancé and a lovely daughter but her dyslexia nagged at her. She had a sense that she was different and disconnected and that no one could really understand what her experience of life was like. And Catherine herself knew she had always struggled to communicate to others what her experience was like, maybe because she had felt a fraud when she was seen as a hero running for help for her mother; and she had never been able to tell anyone "the truth".

Through the EFT sessions we frequently returned to her sense of being different, disconnected and misunderstood. Over time we worked on more details of the memory of finding her mother that Catherine began to recall. Suppressed memories often emerge once the most superficial (i.e. those that are conscious and close to the surface) are acknowledged and cleared. Gradually we were able to release the emotional intensity from many aspects* and parts of this horrific memory; such release occurs when focussing on the memory, naming whatever is known about the feeling and tapping. Scientific research has shown that this release is probably due to changes in the brain activity during tapping (see the websites listed on the final page); what the person experiences is an ability to access the memory without feeling any strong emotion.

In adulthood, Catherine had also developed a real fear of something happening to her health and her daughter being left with no one. Giving herself permission to let go of most of this fear and allowing joy in was a struggle for Catherine as it had become so much a part of her. Her fear fluctuated between that for her own health, which lessened as the sessions progressed, to thoughts and fears associated with her mother's illness and then her death.

Catherine had felt a huge desolation when her mother died and she watched through the window as she was taken away from the house for the last time. She was consumed by the question of who would care for her now that mum was gone and formed a belief which replayed throughout her life that no one ever could or would. Although there have been times that she has let someone get close and has felt loved, her trust in that love is often peppered with doubt and she often fears that others, like colleagues and groups of friends, will not care for or about her. She finds it hard to judge what to say that will be acceptable to others, fearful of the laughter and rejection if she gets it wrong.

Sometimes it is useful to look at what someone might gain out of a habitual behaviour, illness or (repeating) thought. This is not about blaming the person but encouraging honesty and facilitating emotional freedom. We often have reasons to hold on to behaviours that are problematic; many were once a solution, the best we could do at the time to cope with the situation. The current reality may have changed or we may have more resources and could tackle it differently. This is particularly true of solutions we found when we were children. At that time we had little power and few resources unlike our capacity in adulthood to earn money, to move to a different place, to choose who we live with and choose what we do with our time. The beliefs and decisions made by our younger selves are often examples of solutions that might no longer fit. "People are dangerous, I'll withdraw and meet as few of them as possible", may have protected us from a recurrence of abuse but also denies us positive and nurturing relationships and the opportunity to learn how to judge a healthy relationship from an unhealthy one. The belief that "I am alone" may feel acutely true for a child who has lost her mother and is unsure whether her father will have the capacity to look after her alone. But as an adult she has options of finding a partner, friends, contacting relatives, joining groups and communities where she can find connection and care.

One of the subconscious benefits for Catherine of her health anxiety was perhaps that of keeping a connection with, and showing her loyalty to, her mother. Although she would have hated her daughter to go through what she went through, if Catherine became ill she would somehow join with her mother so that she would feel less alone. Or it could assuage a kind of survivor guilt; "She had to suffer and die and I haven't – but it could happen so I don't need to feel so bad about living when mum is dead".

Catherine also realised that her health anxiety meant she thought she would be able to act quickly should anything happen. That's often why we worry; we think that if we do, we will be prepared. However the reality is that either what we're "prepared" for doesn't happen and we've needlessly spent a huge amount of energy and time preoccupied with the worry and mentally preparing for the worst. Or something similar does happen but it's not what we've prepared for; so we do get ill but with a different illness or the misfortune is an accident not an illness at all. Or finally we do get the exact situation we've worried about but we have got it and the years of worrying before were of no help; in fact we may regret wasting all those years being overcautious when we could have lived more fully and have great memories and perhaps greater relationships.

And a third "benefit" or sticking point for Catherine was the anxiety had become who she was, it was a part of her identity. It can be useful, if you want to discover what is holding you in a stuck place, to ask: who would I be, what would I do, what would I think about if not this? Sometimes thinking about one thing prevents us from paying so much attention to something else – it's not necessarily intentional, but we recognise that it 'works' for us so we keep at it. I'm worrying about my future health so I've got no time or energy to think about getting that business off the ground, or getting started on writing that book, or even doing things that might benefit my health. Because it's scary to start the business, it feels exposing and presumptuous to write the book or it takes time and commitment to look after my health. Catherine had worried about her health for so long that she didn't allow herself to think that she might have a long term relationship with her daughter. She had only known her mother for fourteen years, her husband for about five and her fiancé for a few years. Maybe allowing herself to think of being there through many stages of her daughter's life, maybe that was unthinkable. Catherine knew she might actually feel jealous of her daughter if she had a mother throughout her childhood and into adulthood. And she obviously didn't want to feel jealous of her own daughter, so stayed with the thought that she herself would probably die before her daughter reached adulthood. Or she might be angry with her mother for leaving her; again an unthinkable thought when her mother was so important to her. Anger is such a difficult emotion when connected with grief and loss. Fortunately EFT is a great tool for articulating what can't be spoken, for identifying thoughts that have so far remained hidden and for releasing them. Hidden thoughts are not harmless thoughts. They can gnaw away at a person, undermining their sense of self, their self care, nagging at and taking energy from the person. Using EFT to name, acknowledge and release them can be invaluable.

So in our sessions Catherine addressed the "benefits" of her health anxiety, freeing her to think more constructive thoughts such as how she could enjoy life in the present and particularly her relationship with her daughter. Following this she reported enjoying her daughter and their relationship more.

One of the last themes we addressed was Catherine's sense that others didn't and in fact never had appreciated what she had been through and the resources she had had to use and develop. She felt it unfair that others had received advantages because of their own misfortune where Catherine had never even had her experience acknowledged. This played out in two areas of Catherine's life; with her colleagues at work who she felt treated her like a minion and with her partner's ex-wife. This person, who she called her "nemesis" had in fact had a difficult childhood as her mother had taken her own life when she was very young but as Catherine saw it, she had then had her suffering acknowledged and any subsequent problematic behaviour excused or minimised because of this difficult early experience. She had also been taken care of by the authorities thus having her suffering acknowledged. In contrast, Catherine felt no one understood or took account of what she had been through and coped with despite her unbearable grief. EFT and Matrix took Catherine to a place where she was able to honour her own bravery and resourcefulness and from this, talk differently to her colleagues. She brought Wonder Woman into her matrix (the new version of the film was just out at the time we were working together) to show her how to be confident and prepared for life without having always to be vigilant and expect the worst. Not long after our sessions finished, Catherine decided that she was not valued fairly in her current workplace and left, joining somewhere new where she felt she fitted in and had lovely supportive colleagues. She had been able to know that a part of her life didn't honour the person she knew she was and change it for something better. As she mentioned in her feedback, Catherine knew she had spent too long 'pretending' that she was OK. Instead, she decided to change some of what wasn't right and was sapping her energy and take action to enrich her life.

I am still in touch with Catherine and she still uses EFT on herself and in monthly group sessions*. Like all of us, we never "arrive" at a perfect life, we are always (hopefully) learning, developing, and growing, but if we clear some of the big emotional drainers in our lives, the journey is easier and we are able to pause to enjoy the delights along the way.

Catherine fed back to me after our sessions:

"I believe that my sessions with you very much helped me in managing the impact of the chronic childhood trauma I experienced at a young age. Before I came to see you it was as if the past pain was just pushed down under a cover (a fire blanket!) as it certainly was too painful to look at or talk about. If I did I was very selective. Therefore so much energy was spent keeping it covered, pretending I was 'normal' and trying not to let the trauma interfere with everyday life.

With your help I was able to look 'under the cover', see what was there and face it. The tapping took the energy away from the memory and its power to impact my life. I looked at things I never thought I would and in doing so the pain of the memory dissipated. It has helped my relationship with my sisters who experienced the same but I can see they are still locked in the pain; I can be compassionate towards them but know there is a big difference between their experience now and mine."

EFT WITH ANGELA

There wasn't much on her pre-session form; she wanted to tell me in person not on paper. But she did say she had been sexually abused as a child from the age of 4. Child sexual abuse is a difficult topic to even read and think about but if it isn't spoken about, then people who have experienced it may be silenced throughout their lives. So I don't apologise for writing an account of an EFT journey that happened because of an experience of childhood sexual abuse; instead I write it to let people who have experienced it know that they are not alone and it's possible to lessen its impact in adulthood.

When she came, Angela's first comment was that the room had a funny smell. Thankfully it's not my office – I rent a room in the back of a health food shop – so I didn't take it personally! But it did mean I had little control over the room – would the shop owner let me burn incense sticks? Was there any other solution? I was distracted for a moment. But there was nothing I could do right there and then and she was ok to stay, so I just hoped the EFT would distract her!

She told me she wanted to rid herself of an addiction – she didn't say to what – but that it was dominating her life. She didn't know about EFT so I went through my disclaimer and then told her a little about how the session would work. She had tried therapy before and it had worked for a while but not long. She had tried other alternative techniques but to no avail. But she had told her partner that she would die trying if she had to. She knew she needed to rid herself of this addiction.

Angela was a successful business woman with two children she adored. She wasn't with the children's father but had a really strong relationship with her partner with whom she felt totally comfortable. And money was not a problem.

But friendships were. Not because she didn't get on with people but because her addiction meant she needed to be at home every evening. And once she had fed her addiction she couldn't drive, so every evening, even weekend evenings needed to be spent at home. Working during the day meant the only time she could meet with others was weekend lunchtimes and sometimes immediately after school pick up if work allowed. So there was little time to nurture friendships.

Our initial EFT journey lasted 16 sessions and resulted in Angela releasing herself from her addiction. Through recent contact with her, almost 18 months since she stopped taking the substance she was addicted to, she remains free of the addiction that had plagued her and limited her life for years.

At the beginning it was clear that she had been battling this addiction for a long time (she didn't tell me until right at the end what the addiction was, I just knew she had to take/administer/ do the addiction daily). Angela had previously managed to give up but had returned to it. She desperately wanted to be rid of it completely. At times she described herself as a slave to the addiction and she hated the deceit or untruths that accompanied it. She told her children her eyesight wasn't great which was why she could never drive to pick them up when it was dark; she made excuses to friends about not going out in the evenings; and as she was taking an illegal substance, when she went to hotels she always had to check where the security cameras were and where she would be safe from scrutiny.

We began by looking at her current connection with the sexual abuse which finished when she was 12, about 25 years previously. It remained a powerful presence in her life and she was frustrated that she hadn't been able to let it go. She felt shame, disgust, guilt and a sense of catastrophic fear and used food as a comfort. She decided her weight was a way of being unattractive – which was a way of keeping herself safe from her brother. Her older brother was her abuser and also abused her sisters, one of whom became seriously mentally unwell as she got older. We do not know whether there was a connection or whether she would have suffered from mental illness anyway but the experience of abuse may have been very significant. We also touched on, even though it was almost unthinkable, the idea that perhaps her mother had known something.

Tapping focussed on her "ghost bed" memory, an image of her in her bedroom, a ghost of herself, absence from her body being the only way to endure the abuse. We tapped to release her emotional connection with this image and to begin the physical re-connection. With EFT it's possible to approach past traumatic memories gently and safely, once the intensity of even considering facing that memory has reduced to zero or a manageable level. So a person may cry but they are not re-traumatised as people can sometimes feel when simply talking, and not tapping, about a difficult memory. EFT has been shown in research to calm the primitive part of the brain that experiences panic - as if the experience is taking place in the present - and allows other parts of the brain to activate. It's then possible for the person to have a different perspective on the events (for some people they realise the event was only awful because they were a child and seeing it more calmly shows that; they regain a sense of power). In Angela's case, she was able to gain some distance from the events, to separate them from her present consciousness and for her mind to accept that she was not currently in any danger. Matrix Reimprinting was really useful to transform some of her abuse memories, having her mother come into the scene and stop her brother, having the little Angela comfort her sisters and then take them out of the country to a safe place and allowing her little self to say no to her brother. (Of interest to our move to address her unhappiness with her relationship to food at the end of our sessions, in one memory that we changed using Matrix, Angela's mother told the abused younger her to go and have something sweet to eat to make herself feel better while she herself dealt with Angela's brother; but Angela let her know she didn't need food, just a hug. And in the new memory the little Angela was held tightly by her mother. She chose not to use food as a comfort)

Angela realised the addiction may be a way of punishing herself for her perceived crime, her involvement in, and sometimes even excitement at, the sexual acts she had participated in from the age of 4 – albeit because of the power of an older brother. This can be one of the most difficult aspects of abuse; sexual touch can be arousing, exciting and bring physical pleasure even if the person does not invite or understand it and feels scared and angry. And the sufferer can feel special, loved and wanted so at times desires the contact. A drug addiction may have served to replicate some of the stimulating and special feelings related to the abuse for Angela, whilst also being a punishment because it was a means of staying trapped and limited and risking external punishment if caught. We tapped about this, naming the feelings of guilt and shame and letting the younger her know that she was not bad, she was not responsible, she was just a child. EFT also helped Angela reconnect her whole self, the part that felt like a ghost and her physical body.

One session focussed on the power of her brother. Even as an adult Angela rarely mentioned his name. She felt unable to; she was scared of the emotions it would evoke. So gently we worked on this, tapping as she gradually spoke his name in her mind and built up to saying aloud (but quietly) and then saying it loud. On the way home she told me she just kept shouting his name in the car, reclaiming her own power, no longer afraid of the word.

At many points we were addressing Angela's relationship to herself. A core phrase in EFT is "I love and accept myself" (or a variation of that) and it can be really important to say that even if, like many of us, the person doesn't love themselves or struggles with saying that they do. Gradually the repetition of this phrase is a challenge to the perception of the self that Angela, like many other people had, of being disgusting, soiled and tainted. I believe by the end of our sixteen sessions Angela had let go of a great deal of her attachment to believing she was soiled and tainted, but she continued to see herself as disgusting physically because she was overweight and hadn't quite reached a position in which she could treat herself well, could look after herself. This is likely to be an ongoing piece of work that Angela will hopefully be able to undertake at some time.

I am unclear why EFT helps some people more quickly than others. There is the variable of the skill of the practitioner and how quickly they can enable the person to get to the root of the issues identified. Combined with this is the readiness of the client to let go of current patterns and coping mechanisms; EFT can't <u>make</u> anyone do anything; someone might think they want to give up smoking but when they realise it is protecting them from other emotions and decide they don't want to address these emotions, even with a technique as gentle as EFT, then they won't stop smoking. It may be that Angela didn't feel ready to change everything at once and it was enough of a release for her to achieve her goal of giving up her addiction. Or it may be that if I could have found a way for her to feel safer, then she could have totally released the idea that she didn't deserve care within those 16 sessions.

Within an EFT session we often use visual (and other sensory) imagery to depict the emotion. In one session Angela talked about wanting to be free, both of her addiction and in order to live her life. She had a horrible feeling in the pit of her stomach when she thought about not being free and soon pictured this as a monster, tangled inside her, which she knew needed to be destroyed. In that session we managed to shrink the monster but Angela knew she wasn't ready to let it go yet. In effect she still needed to learn something from it, something about being complete in herself. She felt comfort from the addiction and the monster, felt less lonely; for a time it felt like a lifeline that she couldn't live without.

The monster – and the addiction – were also things that were hers. She often wondered what was left for her after giving to others. She held on to this part of her identity because no one could take it away, not her children, her partner, her sisters or her brother. She would take a substance every evening and it was partly her right – I deserve to have something that's mine - and partly it was to feed the monster. In the film "Welcome to Marwen" (trailer here) the protagonist can only move forward when he accepts that his own actions are keeping the nightmare alive. Whilst he takes medication and believes that is the only thing that can save him from the repeating trauma, the agony continues; once he realises that taking the medication is feeding his monster, that he in fact does not need an external prop but can survive this better on his own, he begins to heal. Angela too, at some level, believed that she could not survive, or she would not be treating herself well, if she didn't have her nightly addiction. It was perhaps when some of the intensity of the emotions and the power of the connections with her past were calmed, that she was able to believe in herself and her capacity to survive and in fact live far better than currently, if she no longer fed the addiction/ monster.

Traumatic experiences and their ongoing effects are often viewed as entities to be battled against. We feel we have to be rid of the effects of the trauma by fighting it. In one session however, Angela was able to talk to the monster, to try to understand it rather than simply get rid of it. Her imagined conversation with the monster led her to the realisation that the addiction – to the substance, to food and to the trauma of the abuse – were reasons for her to abdicate responsibility for her own life. If she let go of these monsters, she would have to make decisions about her life, what she wanted to feed herself, how she wanted to view herself, what she wanted to do with her evenings, and she understood she was frightened of taking responsibility in case she failed. It was easier – in some ways - to have her life dictated by her history and her addictions rather than choose to look at herself and know that she deserved to be fed well, to be free to use her evenings as she wished, to have a body she felt happy with that didn't slow her down, to know that she was "good enough", absolutely fine as she was rather than a tainted, disgusting little girl who couldn't be trusted or looked after.

In one session we worked with the idea of Angela forgiving herself. This again can be a difficult concept with any trauma, especially abuse; the little Angela clearly had nothing to be forgiven for. However Angela had spent much of her life trying to make up for what she considered her failings as a child. With her own children she made a commitment to protect them from all danger. She did this brilliantly but it was perhaps at her own expense because it was exhausting – something that fed into her need to have her special treat at the end of the day. She also felt guilty that she had not protected her sisters. Again this was not her responsibility but it's often important to send forgiveness to our younger selves because we trap ourselves in some degree of guilt and blame. We can add that there is nothing that needs forgiving, but our younger selves will often pipe up with a riposte, claiming that he or she did this or that wrong. Gently acknowledging the sense of guilt and those mistakes that we all inevitably make along the way and allowing our younger selves the reassurance that all is forgiven and released, can be a really important step for many people. For a while Angela's monster became more fluid and almost a protector, an ally rather than an enemy when we tapped to offer her younger self forgiveness.

In another session Angela really focussed on the pleasure she had experienced during the abuse, particularly in the sweets she received afterwards. She felt a ball of disgust in her stomach thinking of this but through the EFT the ball disappeared and she moved into loving rather than despising herself. This also gave space for her own mother to enter the matrix imagery and offer the child Angela love as well.

It was after 10 sessions that Angela decided she was ready to give up her addiction. At that point she told me her addiction was to cannabis. She and her partner arranged a week off work, made plans for the children to be looked after and booked into a local hotel. She didn't take any cannabis with her, booked a couple of acupuncture sessions, found an addiction support group she was allowed to drop in to and we planned four further sessions in the hotel. Angela anticipated she would need all this support in that first week but in actual fact needed far less than she had thought. We only needed two sessions. I also saw Angela again a couple of weeks later. We did some work on her realising that her addiction had had a big impact on her partner and maybe for the first time she acknowledged it had had an impact on her children too; she had hidden it from them and protected them from it, but she was able to acknowledge that it had still had an impact. We tapped focussing on her sadness that she allowed the addiction to have an impact for so long but through the tapping realised she had not intended to cause harm – in fact she had tried to minimise it. She became calmer and less distressed once she realised this.

Angela felt she had done enough work by this stage. She had achieved her goal of freeing herself of her addiction. She knew there was more work to be done – I think we have things to work on throughout our lives; the job is never finished. However there are times that intense focussed work should be done and times life should just be enjoyed. Angela was able to live life more freely, take her girls places in the evenings, and, perhaps principally, feel free of the threat that had hung over her for so long.

T O CONCLUDE

You have now read the EFT stories of four women – and it could easily have been four men.

So what about you?

Do you feel you're not good enough as Annabel did?
Do you feel you're not really true to yourself, living the life you want to be living like Claire?
Do you feel you're different, like Catherine?
Do you feel angry as Angela did?

Is there something else that holds you back from living life as fully as you want? Others I have worked with have been held back by a recent relationship trauma (Graham), by extreme self criticism and anorexia following an abortion of which she felt so ashamed (Hannah), by a sense that his parents didn't love him resulting in life-long self punishment (Steve) and by the acutely painful and dismissive comments of an alcoholic father leaving a legacy of self harm and bulimia (Sasha).

All have been helped by EFT and Matrix.

There are so many online videos and audios that might help you – why not give one or two a try? You only have a little bit of time to lose and so much to gain. Just google EFT for ... whatever your issue is (anxiety, depression, weight loss, public speaking etc etc)

And it you'd like to contact me please do: hello@tapyourtroublesaway.uk

Tanya

www.tapyourtroublesaway.uk

EFT RESEARCH

The best places to find current research are on the websites for EFT International https://eftinternational.org/ and EFT Universe https://www.eftuniverse.com. The Association for Comprehensive Energy Psychology (ACEP) website also lists research papers for EFT and other techniques that are categorised as energy psychology or energy therapy -https://www.energypsych.org/